In the Name of Luminosity
and Transparency

## ODYSSEUS ELYTIS
1979 NOBEL PRIZE FOR LITERATURE

# In the Name of
# Luminosity
## and
# Transparency

Introduction:
Dimitris Daskalopoulos

AIORA

The English translation of Elytis' Nobel lecture was provided by the Nobel Foundation. His speech at the Nobel banquet and Dimitris Daskalopoulos' essay "The poet Odysseus Elytis" were translated into English by Simon Darragh, from French and Greek respectively.

© The Nobel Foundation 1979
© for this edition, Aiora Press 2016

ISBN: 978-618-5048-51-8

AIORA PRESS
11 Mavromichali st.
Athens 10679, Greece
tel: +30 210 3839000
**www.aiora.gr**

The Nobel Prize in Literature 1979
was awarded to Odysseus Elytis
"for his poetry, which, against
the background of Greek tradition,
depicts with sensuous strength
and intellectual clear-sightedness
modern man's struggle for
freedom and creativeness."

# Contents

# Introduction
# The Poet Odysseus Elytis

The shot that was heard on the afternoon of the 21st of July 1928 in the seashore area of Agios Spyridon in Preveza took on, with the passage of time, symbolic significance. The suicide of the poet K.G. Karyotakis marked the end of the tired and clumsy Greek poetry of the first decades of the 20th century, which had for some time supported what was known as "Karyotakism" and at the same time prepared the way for the new modern poetry which was to appear a few years later. A month before that fateful afternoon, Odysseus, the last child of the Alepoudelis family, had received his secondary school-leaving certificate. Both his parents came from Mytilene, though from different villages. His father, Panayiotis Alepoudelis, settled in Heraklion, Crete, in 1895, where, with his brother, he founded a soap and kernel-oil factory, which they moved to Piraeus in 1914, and the family stayed in Athens. The couple had six children. The poet was born in Heraklion at dawn on the 2nd of November 1911.

From the beginning of the 20th century the leading figure in Greek poetry had been Kostis Palamas, in whose shadow the more modern generation of poets came to maturity. After the First World War a poetic style had already been established that, both in subject-matter and expression, repeated fixed, unoriginal motifs. It was already apparent that renewal was needed. It is worth noting that the group of poets who would soon import and follow the new movement that was being formed in European countries had spent some time in them, were polyglot, and came from urban families. On the other hand, those who followed a left-wing ideology stayed faithful to traditional poetry, and thought modernism contrary to their beliefs. The Alexandrian poet C.P. Cavafy who after the Second World War was about to emerge as a figure of international standing, was nevertheless a controversial case. Karyotakis was precisely on the watershed between old and modern poetry, with his emphatic language, obvious irony, and tendency to transcend the quotidian.

Such was the climate in which Elytis, who never took an interest in his father's trade, grew up. When he finished his secondary education he agreed, obviously because of its connection with his father's profession, to study chemistry. Ultimately he changed to law, though he never took a degree. He had been writing poems since his school days, and published them under a variety of pseudonyms in the long-lived periodical *I Diaplasis ton Paidon*, as had many of his predecessors and as would many future generations of lovers of the muse. Apart from this, his commitment to poetry was not yet decisive. As he wrote in his revealing text "The Chronicle of a Decade" (in *Open Papers*), poetry didn't "say much" to him at that time: from school books "I got the vague impression that it was no more than a verbose and boring rhythm-chopping. Poems were used to talk of mountains and rivers and to call them commonplace. Besides, our teachers presented them as something only needed for the June exams." Still a student, seeking another opinion and a different content for poetry, he would admit that the language of Karyotakis "Was without doubt a new language", while in C.P. Cavafy he saw "wrinkles" despite Cavafy's own intention to exorcise, by any means necessary, the old ways of the world... New horizons opened for him when a book by Paul Eluard came into his hands. In a very short time after that decisive moment, Odysseus Alepoudelis started to change into Odysseus Elytis, who would make his mark on contemporary Greek poetry, opening new vistas of expression.

The anecdotal but genuinely eventful story of how G.K. Katsimbalis forced the first important public appearance of Elytis, in the periodical *Ta Nea Grammata* (The New Letters) in 1935, has been written by the poet himself, and has been vouched for by other witnesses. The year 1935 is also well-known as one —important for modern poetry—in which the periodical *Ta Nea Grammata* started to circulate: the periodical round which rallied poets and prose writers of about the same age; the so-called "Generation of the 1930s". It published Georgios Seferis' poetry collection *Novel* and the collection *Blast Furnace* by the surrealist Andreas Embirikos, who thus marked that same year by his notorious choice of surrealism. Before the end of 1935 Elytis published his first poems.

We know today that in those years only a very limited circle of readers read modern poetry: such poets as went away from rhyme and known metres were lumped together as surrealists. Elytis began with surrealism, but he didn't submit his poetry to the severe prescriptions of the movement. He travelled with it for a while, borrowed its elements and transformed them, according to his own lights, into a reasoned and linguistically breath-taking lyricism. He preserved the excesses of surrealism and they are impressed clearly on Elytis' pictorial collages, which he valued highly, regarding them as another expression of his poetry, calling them "Syneikones" (Collages).

Elytis' relations to the pictorial arts are long and deep. They are not exhausted by the multitude of pictures in his poetry, but are also shown in his Collages, and in the relations he formed and maintained with great European and Greek visual artists. It is worth noting that there is always a frontispiece in colour of a painting in his poetry collections. Furthermore, many of his shorter writings are aesthetic analyses of works by Greek and foreign artists. He himself has said "My interest in the visual arts existed earlier. It was always great. I flatter myself to think that if I had not become a poet, I could have been a good painter... and so, to give some reality to my wishes, I turned my attention in the direction of collage... This had first been done by Max Ernst, in the midst of surrealism, conjoining various pictures from old engravings and making very unusual compositions... Using present-day photography, and indeed chiefly with Greek materials, whatever I could find—seas, girls, icons—I made some compositions that I called Syneikones (Collages)."

His vocabulary has no match in our modern writing. The poetry of Cavafy, for instance, like that of Seferis, was written using about 3,500 words. Elytis uses more than twice this number; nearly 8,000! His poetry brings an air of health, daring, and light as a necessary resistance, at least in his first period, to "Karyotakism"; as an affirmation of life. His previous characterization as a "Poet of the Aegean" (which he himself later found sadly limiting) cannot in fact be made to correspond with his whole creative career, but this doesn't contradict the fact that he "discovered" the Aegean as a poetic theme and, at the same time, as the place in which ancient Greek lyric poetry first flowered with his "distant cousin" Sappho.

Before the outbreak of war in 1940, Elytis had published a series of his poems and translations, had studied the theoretical texts of foreign surrealists, had associated with the circle of poets and prose writers of the periodical *Ta Nea Grammata* and had made friends with Andreas Embirikos, with whom he had travelled through Greece discovering both characteristic and until then unnoticed aspects of Greece and its traditions. Before he enlisted as a reserve second lieutenant at the front, *Orientations* was published: a book which consolidates his individuality of both language and expression, and shows his power in creating images. The experiences, hardships, and atmosphere of the war would be brought to fruition in his collection of poems *Heroic and Elegiac Song for the Lost Second Lieutenant of Albania* in the yet unpublished *Alvaniada* (Albanian Epic), in the also unpublished *I kalosyni stis lykopories* (Kindness in the Wolf Lairs) and, finally, they would return in the first part of the composition *The Axion Esti* in which individual and collective fates are brought together and treated as identical.

The publication of *The Axion Esti* and its simultaneous circulation with the collection *Six and One Remorses for the Sky* interrupted a period of silence in poetry on the part of Elytis that had lasted about fifteen years (1945-1960). In that period the poet may not have published new poems, but he wrote theoretical and short prose works, worked with the newspaper *I Kathimerini* as an art critic, travelled in France and England, where he met newly appearing poets and representational artists, and translated theatrical works (*Ondine* by Giraudoux, *The Caucasian Chalk Circle* by Brecht, *The Maids* by Genet).

*The Axion Esti* brings together and completes many of the virtues of Elytis' so far twenty-five year long creative career: it aspires at the same time to express, in a synthesis unusual in modern Greek poetry, the extent and architectonic completeness of individual and national consciousness. The highly vigorous nature of the work is precisely the extremely studied architectonics which distinguish its three parts ("Genesis", "The Passion", "The Axion Esti").

The complete balance between them, the harmonised arrangement of the verses, the breaks between the hemistichs (marked typographically in the book itself), the regularly spaced interpositions of prose "Readings", the habitual return of certain verse forms: all these, expressed in word-pictures, yield and bring forth a perseveringly and patiently finished composition of rhythmic harmony. Here, the organization of poetic material reaches its apotheosis, without however restricting poetic freedom and expression in pre-arranged forms. Another feature that lends especial charm to the whole work is the deliberate use of the expressions and forms of the orthodox church tradition, which thus emphasises the close ties between Greekness and orthodoxy. The musical settings of selections from *The Axion Esti* by the composer Mikis Theodorakis endeared it to the general public, made it its own, and contributed to the broadening of its accessibility. In spite of all this, and apart from its perceptible influences on younger poets, it cannot be considered a pioneering work of poetry, rather a fortunate moment of severely studied conception and rendition.

The decade 1960-1970 was for Elytis a new period of public silence in poetry, which came to an end in 1971 with the publication of his collection *The Light Tree and the Fourteenth Beauty*. His publishing activities increased year by year: up to the time of his winning the Nobel Prize he had published the poetry books *The Light Tree and the Fourteenth Beauty*; the short prose works *The Painter Theophilos* (1973), *Open Papers* (1974), *The Spell of Papadiamandis* (1976), *Report to Andreas Embirikos* (1978) and the volume of translations of foreign poets *Defteri grafi* (Second Writing) (1976). Most of these had kept the poet busy during the previous years, showing that his period of silence had in fact been fertile. But such books as have been published since his winning of the Nobel Prize have also shown this delay between writing and publication, a characteristic case being *The Little Mariner*, parts of which had already been published in 1976, while the complete book appeared in 1985. Elytis' first collection of poems after the Nobel, *Three poems under a Flag of Convenience* was almost unmentioned critically, while on the contrary the obviously shorter but richly meaningful *Journal of an Unseen April* had provoked considered critical comment; this was a peak moment for the poet in the 1980s. His penultimate collection before his death *The Oxopetra Elegies* had also provoked extensive critical writing, and this collection, together with *West of Sorrow* (1995) and the posthumous *Ek tou plision* (From Nearby) (1998) proved his youthful creative vigour. In fact, he was the only one of

Greece's major 20th century poets who was lucky enough to be long-lived and continue to create up to the eve of his death.

Many of his books in the period 1971-78 are prose works: essays, to which must be added *Carte Blanche* (1992), a volume corresponding in length and content to *Open Papers*, *O kipos me tis aftapates* (The Garden of Self-delusions) (1995) and the microscopic *2χ7ε* (1996). Elytis' essays are far from what we would call classic essays, chiefly because of their poetic language, which is nearer poetic expression rather than reasoned argument. But in any case, his related texts are consistent with the ideology of his general cosmology, the basic tenets of which are "The metaphysics of the sun", the revealing of the miraculous in everyday life, the lasting fascination of Greece as a place, and historical memory and tradition. Elytis' essays are clearly poetic texts, and the reflections of the person who wrote them carry the reader on charming waves of words, as if in an extended poem.

The sum of his offerings has been recognized with many honours. Apart from the State Prize, which was awarded for *The Axion Esti*, he was given a doctorate by the University of Thessaloniki (before the Nobel), and a crowd of people attended his funeral, which in accordance with his wishes was without formal announcement or funeral orations. The announcement by the Swedish Academy when awarding him the Nobel Prize for Literature in 1979 declared in a pithy and timely way the value of his work: "For his poetry, which, against the background of Greek tradition, depicts with sensuous strength and intellectual clear-sightedness modern man's struggle for freedom and creativeness."

Dimitris Daskalopoulos
Athens, November 2015

# A Thirst for Miracles

*Elytis' speech at the Nobel Banquet, December 10, 1979*

Your Majesties, Your Highnesses, Members of the Academy, Ladies and Gentlemen:

The journey of Odysseus—whose name I happen to have been given—never ends, it would seem. And that is fortunate. One of our greatest contemporary poets told us that the deepest meaning of the journey isn't the arrival in Ithaca, which is a finishing, an end: it's the journey itself; the adventures and the learning.

Man's need to discover, to understand, to make myths about all that surpasses him seems incurable. We all have a thirst for miracles; an urge to believe in miracles; all we have to do is to be ready; to wait. I, in my turn, in devoting more than forty years of my life to poetry, did nothing else. I crossed mythical seas, stopping at, and getting to know so many places.

And, lo and behold, here I am today in Stockholm, my only treasure a few Greek words. Humble words but alive, because they are on the lips of a whole people. They are three thousand years old, but as fresh as if just drawn from the sea, from the pebbles and sea-weed of an Aegean shore: from the deep blue and total transparency of the æther. The word "Ouranos" (sky); the word "Thalassa" (sea); the word "Helios" (sun) and the word "Eleftheria" (freedom). I lay them respectfully at your feet. To thank you; to thank the generous people of Sweden and their leading intellectuals who, turning away from majority criteria, show every year that they have that secret ability to renew the Miracle.

Thank you.

# In the Name of Luminosity and Transparency

*Elytis' Nobel Lecture, December 8, 1979*

May I please be allowed to speak in the name of luminosity and transparency. The space I have lived in and where I have been able to fulfill myself is defined by these two states. States that I have also perceived as being identified in me with the need to express myself.

It is good, it is right that a contribution be made to art, from that which is assigned to each individual by his personal experience and the virtues of his language. Even more so, since the times are dismal and we should have the widest possible view of things.

I am not speaking of the common and natural capacity of perceiving objects in all their detail, but of the power of the metaphor to only retain their essence, and to bring them to such a state of purity that their metaphysical significance appears like a revelation.

I am thinking here of the manner in which the sculptors of the Cycladic period[1] used their material, to the point of carrying it beyond itself. I am also thinking of the Byzantine icon painters, who succeeded, only by using pure color, to suggest the "divine".

It is just such an intervention in the real, both penetrating and metamorphosing, which has always been, it seems to me, the lofty vocation of poetry. Not limiting itself to what is, but stretching itself to what can be. It is true that this step has not always been received with respect. Perhaps the collective neuroses did not permit it. Or perhaps because utilitarianism did not authorize men to keep their eyes open as much as was necessary.

Beauty, Light, it happens that people regard them as obsolete, as insignificant. And yet! The inner step required by the approach of the Angel's form is, in my opinion, infinitely more painful than the other, which gives birth to Demons of all kinds.

Certainly, there is an enigma. Certainly, there is a mystery. But the mystery is not a stage piece turning to account the play of light and shadow only to impress us.

It is what continues to be a mystery, even in bright light. It is only then that it acquires that refulgence that captivates, which we call Beauty. Beauty that is an open path—the only one perhaps—towards that unknown part of ourselves, towards that which surpasses us. There, this could be yet another definition of poetry: the art of approaching that which surpasses us.

Innumerable secret signs, with which the universe is studded and which constitute so many syllables of an unknown language, urge us to compose words, and with words, phrases whose deciphering puts us at the threshold of the deepest truth.

In the final analysis, where is truth? In the erosion and death we see around us, or in this propensity to believe that the world is indestructible and eternal? I know, it is wise to avoid redundancies. The cosmogonic theories that have succeeded each other through the years have not missed using and abusing them. They have clashed among themselves, they have had their moment of glory, then they have been erased.

But the essential has remained. It remains.

The poetry that raises itself when rationalism has laid down its arms, takes its relieving troops to advance into the forbidden zone, thus proving that it is still the less consumed by erosion. It assures, in the purity of its form, the safeguard of those given facts through which life becomes a viable task. Without it and its vigilance, these given facts would be lost in the obscurity of consciousness, just as algae become indistinct in the ocean depths.

That is why we have a great need of transparency. To clearly perceive the knots of this thread running throughout the centuries and aiding us to remain upright on this earth.

These knots, these ties, we see them distinctly, from Heraclitus[2] to Plato[3] and from Plato to Jesus. Having reached us in various forms they tell us the same thing: that it is in the inside of this world that the other world is contained, that it is with the elements of this world that the other world is recombined, the hereafter, that second reality situated above the one where we live unnaturally. It is a question of a reality to which we have a total right, and only our incapacity makes us unworthy of it.

It is not a coincidence that in healthy times, Beauty is identified with Good, and Good with the Sun. To the extent that consciousness purifies itself and is filled with light, its dark portions retract and disappear, leaving empty spaces that—just as in the laws of physics—are filled by the elements of the opposite import. Thus what results of this rests on the two aspects, I mean the "here" and the "hereafter". Did not Heraclitus speak of a harmony of opposed tensions?

It is of no importance whether it is Apollo[4] or Venus,[5] Christ or the Virgin who incarnate and personalize the need we have to see materialized what we experience as an intuition. What is important is the breath of immortality that penetrates us at that moment. In my humble opinion, Poetry should, beyond all doctrinal argumentation, permit this breath.

Here I must refer to Hölderlin,[6] that great poet who looked at the gods of Olympus and Christ in the same manner. The stability he gave a kind of vision continues to be inestimable. And the extent of what he has revealed for us is immense. I would even say it is terrifying. It is what incites us to cry out—at a time when the pain now submerging us was just beginning—: "What good are poets in a time of poverty". *Wozu Dichter in dürftiger Zeit?*

For mankind, times were always *dürftig*, unfortunately. But poetry has never, on the other hand, missed its vocation. These are two facts that will never cease to accompany our earthly destiny, the first serving as the counter-weight to the other. How could it be otherwise? It is through the Sun that the night and the stars are perceptible to us. Yet let us note, with the ancient sage, that if it passes its bounds the Sun becomes ὕβρις ("hubris"). For life to be possible, we have to keep a correct distance to the allegorical Sun, just as our planet does from the natural Sun. We formerly erred through ignorance. We go wrong today through the extent of our knowledge. In saying this I do not wish to join the long list of censors of our technological civilization. Wisdom as old as the country from which I come has taught me to accept evolution, to digest progress "with its bark and its pits".

But then, what becomes of Poetry? What does it represent in such a society? This is what I reply: poetry is the only place where the power of numbers proves to be nothing. Your decision this year to honor, in my person, the poetry of a small country, reveals the relationship of harmony linking it to the concept of gratuitous art, the only concept that opposes nowadays the all-powerful position acquired by the quantitative esteem of values.

Referring to personal circumstances would be a breach of good manners. Praising my home, still more unsuitable. Nevertheless it is sometimes indispensable, to the extent that such interferences assist in seeing a certain state of things more clearly. This is the case today.

Dear friends, it has been granted to me to write in a language that is spoken only by a few million people. But a language spoken without interruption, with very few differences, throughout more than two thousand five hundred years. This apparently surprising spatial-temporal distance is found in the cultural dimensions of my country. Its spatial area is one of the smallest; but its temporal extension is infinite. If I remind you of this, it is certainly not to derive some kind of pride from it, but to show the difficulties a poet faces when he must make use, to name the things dearest to him, of the same words as did Sappho,[7] for example, or Pindar,[8] while being deprived of the audience they had and which then extended to all of human civilization.

If language were not such a simple means of communication there would not be any problem. But it happens, at times, that it is also an instrument of "magic". In addition, in the course of centuries, language acquires a certain way of being. It becomes a lofty speech. And this way of being entails obligations.

Let us not forget either that in each of these twenty-five centuries and without any interruption, poetry has been written in Greek. It is this collection of given facts which makes the great weight of tradition that this instrument lifts. Modern Greek poetry gives an expressive image of this.

The sphere formed by this poetry shows, one could say, two poles: at one of these poles is Dionysios Solomos,[9] who, before Mallarmé appeared in European literature, managed to formulate, with the greatest rigor and coherency, the concept of pure poetry: to submit sentiment to intelligence, ennoble expression, mobilize all the possibilities of the linguistic instrument by orienting oneself to the miracle. At the other pole is Cavafy,[10] who like T.S. Eliot reaches, by eliminating all form of turgidity, the extreme limit of concision and the most rigorously exact expression.

Between these two poles, and more or less close to one or the other, our other great poets move: Kostis Palamas,[11] Angelos Sikelianos,[12] Nikos Kazantzakis,[13] George Seferis.[14]

Such is, rapidly and schematically drawn, the picture of neo-Hellenic poetic discourse.

We who have followed have had to take over the lofty precept which has been bequeathed to us and adapt it to contemporary sensibility. Beyond the limits of technique, we have had to reach a synthesis, which, on the one hand, assimilated the elements of Greek tradition and, on the other, the social and psychological requirements of our time.

In other words, we had to grasp today's European-Greek in all its truth and turn that truth to account. I do not speak of successes, I speak of intentions, efforts. Orientations have their significance in the investigation of literary history.

But how can creation develop freely in these directions when the conditions of life, in our time, annihilate the creator? And how can a cultural community be created when the diversity of languages raises an unsurpassable obstacle? We know you and you know us through the 20 or 30 per cent that remains of a work after translation. This holds even more true for all those of us who, prolonging the furrow traced by Solomos, expect a miracle from discourse and that a spark flies from between two words with the right sound and in the right position.

No. We remain mute, incommunicable.

We are suffering from the absence of a common language. And the consequences of this absence can be seen—I do not believe I am exaggerating—even in the political and social reality of our common homeland, Europe.

We say—and make the observation each day—that we live in a moral chaos. And this at a moment when—as never before—the allocation of that which concerns our material existence is done in the most systematic manner, in an almost military order, with implacable controls. This contradiction is significant. Of two parts of the body, when one is hypertrophic, the other atrophies. A praise-worthy tendency, encouraging the peoples of Europe to unite, is confronted today with the impossibility of harmonization of the atrophied and hypertrophic parts of our civilization. Our values do not constitute a common language.

For the poet—this may appear paradoxical but it is true—the only common language he still can use is his sensations. The manner in which two bodies are attracted to each other and unite has not changed for millennia. In addition, it has not given rise to any conflict, contrary to the scores of ideologies that have bloodied our societies and have left us with empty hands.

When I speak of sensations, I do not mean those, immediately perceptible, on the first or second level. I mean those which carry us to the extreme edge of ourselves. I also mean the "analogies of sensations" that are formed in our spirits.

For all art speaks through analogy. A line, straight or curved, a sound, sharp or low-pitched, translate a certain optical or acoustic contact. We all write good or bad poems to the extent that we live or reason according to the good or bad meaning of the term. An image of the sea, as we find it in Homer, comes to us intact. Rimbaud will say "a sea mixed with sun". Except he will add: "that is eternity." A young girl holding a myrtle branch in Archilochus[15] survives in a painting by Matisse. And thus the Mediterranean idea of purity is made more tangible to us. In any case, is the image of a virgin in Byzantine iconography so different from that of her secular sisters? Very little is needed for the light of this world to be transformed into supernatural clarity, and inversely. One sensation inherited from the Ancients and another bequeathed by the Middle Ages give birth to a third, one that resembles them both, as a child does its parents. Can poetry survive such a path? Can sensations, at the end of this incessant purification process, reach a state of sanctity? They will return then, as analogies, to graft themselves on the material world and to act on it.

It is not enough to put our dreams into verse. It is too little. It is not enough to politicize our speech. It is too much. The material world is really only an accumulation of materials. It is for us to show ourselves to be good or bad architects, to build Paradise or Hell. This is what poetry never ceases affirming to us—and particularly in these dürftiger times—just this: that in spite of everything our destiny lies in our hands.

I have often tried to speak of solar metaphysics. I will not try today to analyse how art is implicated in such a conception. I will keep to one single and simple fact: the language of the Greeks, like a magic instrument, has—as a reality or a symbol—intimate relations with the Sun. And that Sun does not only inspire a certain attitude of life, and hence the primeval sense to the poem. It penetrates the composition, the structure, and—to use a current terminology—the nucleus from which is composed the cell we call the poem.

It would be a mistake to believe that it is a question of a return to the notion of pure form. The sense of form, as the West has bequeathed it to us, is a constant attainment, represented by three or four models. Three or four moulds, one could say, where it was suitable to pour the most anomalous material at any price. Today that is no longer conceivable. I was one of the first in Greece to break those ties.

What interested me, obscurely at the beginning, then more and more consciously, was the use of that material according to an architectural model that varied each time. To understand this there is no need to refer to the wisdom of the Ancients who conceived their Parthenons. It is enough to evoke the humble builders of our houses and of our chapels in the Cyclades, finding on each occasion the best solution. Their solutions. Practical and beautiful at the same time, so that in seeing them Le Corbusier could only admire and bow down.

Perhaps it is this instinct that awakened in me when, for the first time, I had to face a great composition like "The Axion Esti." I understood then that without giving the work the proportions and perspective of an edifice, it would never reach the solidity I wished.

I followed the example of Pindar or of the Byzantine Romanos Melodos[16] who, in each of their odes or canticles, invented a new mode for each occasion. I saw that the determined repetition, at intervals, of certain elements of versification effectively gave to my work that multifaceted and symmetrical substance which was my plan.

But then is it not true that the poem, thus surrounded by elements that gravitate around it, is transformed into a little Sun? This perfect correspondence, which I thus find obtained with the intended contents, is, I believe, the poet's most lofty ideal.

To hold the Sun in one's hands without being burned, to transmit it like a torch to those following, is a painful act but, I believe, a blessed one. We have need of it. One day the dogmas that hold men in chains will be dissolved before a consciousness so inundated with light that it will be one with the Sun, and it will arrive on those ideal shores of human dignity and liberty.

1. Cycladic Art: The earliest form of ancient Greek art. Its peak was three thousand years B.C., in the Bronze Age. Its characteristic examples are small statuettes (the so-called "eidolia"), ceramics and pottery. It developed in most of the islands of the Aegean archipelago, the group known as the Cyclades, using the raw materials of the islands: obsidian, corundum, marble. The formal configuration and simplicity of line is very much comparable with the abstraction of modern art.

2. Heraclitus: Important pre-Socratic philosopher of the sixth century B.C. Only fragments of his work have survived.

3. Plato (c.427-348/347 B.C.): Great ancient Greek philosopher. Student of Socrates, whose teachings he set forth in his writings. He and Aristotle are the founding pillars of later western philosophical thought.

4. Apollo: One of the twelve Olympian Gods of Ancient Greece. The God of light, music, and lyric poetry; thus he is often represented holding a lyre. His life and appearance have been a favourite theme, especially in the painting and sculpture of the romantic era.

5. Venus (Aphrodite): Goddess of Beauty and Love among the twelve Gods of ancient Greece. Her form has been represented in countless paintings, while her most famous sculptural representation is the so-called "Venus of Milo", which is in the Louvre in Paris.

6. Friedrich Hölderlin (1770-1843): Among the most important lyric poets in the German language. A large part of his total output (poetry and drama) draws its inspiration from ancient Greece. The most famous of his works are the novel *Hyperion* and the uncompleted drama *The Death of Empedocles*.

7. Sappho (c.630-570 B.C.): Famous lyric poet from Mytilene (Lesbos). Hers was among the first poetic voices to express personal feelings, with the main theme being the trials and sufferings of erotic love.

8. Pindar (522/518-c.438 B.C.): Leading lyric poet of ancient times. Wrote hymns to the winners of the PanHellenic games (Olympic, Isthmian, Nemean etc.). Only four relatively complete books of his have survived, known as the *Victory Odes*.

9. Dionysios Solomos (1789-1857): Leading figure and progenitor of Modern Greek Poetry. His most important poetic works were uncompleted, but in spite of that show his poetic genius. Many of his poems were inspired by the revolution of 1821. Verses from his extended poem "Hymn to Liberty" are used as the Greek National Anthem.

10. C.P. Cavafy (1863-1933): The most translated and best known Greek poet internationally. His work exists in multiple translations in a wide range of languages. Was born and died in Alexandria, Egypt, where a Greek community flourished from the mid nineteenth century on.

11. Kostis Palamas (1859-1943): Key figure of the Generation of the 1880s; poet, essayist, playwright, historian and critic, regarded as one of Greece's leading lights, significantly contributed to modern Greek poetry's development and renewal. His funeral, during the German occupation, assumed the character of an act of resistance, in defiance of the presence of German troops at the cemetery and the prevalent climate of fear, with the huge crowd gathered there chanting the national anthem of Greece.

12. Angelos Sikelianos (1884-1951): Among the most important Greek poets of the 20th century. Together with his American wife Eva Palmer he organized the Delphic Festivals in 1927 and 1930. Held in great esteem by Seferis,

who mentioned him frequently in his diaries and wrote essays about his work.

13. Nikos Kazantzakis (1883-1957): Prolific writer, whose strong philosophical, religious and social struggles have marked most of his work. Wrote impressions of his worldwide travels, theatrical works, the lengthy epic "Odysseus" (33,333 verses), but became known world wide for his novels, written in the last years of his life. Two of them, *The Life and Times of Alexis Zorbas* (Zorba the Greek) and *The Last Temptation*, also achieved fame as films.

14. George Seferis (1900-1971): The first Greek to be awarded the Nobel Prize for Literature (1963). Leading figure in the so-called "Generation of the 1930s", whose poets renewed contemporary Greek poetry. Was a career diplomat, and left a long and varied selection of written works: poetry, memoirs, letters, essays, translations of foreign writers and a novel. His poetry expresses the long course of Hellenism and his essays are models of linguistic clarity and purity.

15. Archilochus (c.712-c.664 B.C.): The supreme lyric poet of the ancient Greek world. His surviving poems are clear expressions of personal life, removed from the mythical and epic poetry of his time. An important influence on later poets.

16. Romanos the Melodist: Biographical details are unclear, but he must have lived, so received wisdom has it, in the sixth century A.D. in Syria. He is considered the greatest Byzantine hymnographer in church poetry

# Chronology of Elytis' life

**1911**  Birth of Odysseus Alepoudelis (2nd of November) in Herakleion, Crete; the last of the six children of Panayiotis and Maria Alepoudelis. The father of the poet has a soap factory, which he moves to Piraeus in 1914, and all the family settles in Athens. The second of November was commemorated by the posthumous publication of the short text *2χ7ε*, also that of the collection *From Nearby*.

**1919-25**  In these years the Alepoudeli family spends the summers in Spetses, where the young Odysseus comes into direct contact with island and sea life—themes which would appear emphatically later in his poems. This carefree youthful time is marred by two deaths: on the last day of 1918 Myrsini, the family's first child and only daughter, dies in her 20th year in the Spanish Flu epidemic, and his father dies in the summer of 1925.

1928   General education ends, and he prepares to take exams and study chemistry. He has already started to study poetry, and he changes direction and enrols in the Law School of Athens University, without completing his studies.

1934   Writes his first poems, which would be published later in the collection *Orientations*. Becomes acquainted with the circle of poets around the periodical *Ta Nea Grammata* (New Letters) and, at the same time, translates French poets (Paul Eluard and Pierre Jean Jouve).

1935   In spite of his initial objections, he allows his poems to be published in *Ta Nea Grammata* and chooses, instead of his family name, the pseudonym Elytis.

1937-38   Does his military service in Kerkyra, where he will meet the doctor, marine biologist and translator of Greek poetry Theodore Stephanides and the English writer Lawrence Durrell.

1940   His first book of poetry *Orientations* is printed: a collection of his published output to date. Studies and criticisms of his poems are published. When war breaks out he serves as a reserve second lieutenant on the northern borders of Greece.

1941   Is taken to hospital in Ioannina in critical condition with typhus. With the entry of the Germans into Greece he is taken to Athens, still unwell. Starts to write poetry again.

**1943**    The collection *Sun the First* appears.

**1945**    *Poèmes*, a selection of his poems translated into French by Robert Levesque in co-operation with G.K. Katsimbalis, is printed by the Athens French Institute. He is appointed director of the newly formed National Radio Foundation, a position he abandons the next year.

**1946**    Meeting and acquaintance with the French poet Paul Eluard, who is in Athens. Also becomes acquainted with the English publisher and journalist John Lehmann. 1946-49 was a period of civil war in Greece.

**1947**    His long poem *I kalosyni stis lykopories* (Kindness in the Wolf Lairs) is published in the periodical *Mikro Tetradio* (Little Notebook); a poem that has not appeared until now in any collection and has never been published in full. Translates Lorca's *Romancero Gitano*. Travels in the liberated—and finally incorporated into Greece—Dodecanese islands. Tries unsuccessfully to get a passport in order to travel to France. Robert Levesque's book *Domaine Grec*, in which Elytis and others are anthologised, is published in Athens. The book provokes recriminations in Athenian literary circles.

**1948**   Finally obtains a passport and travels abroad: Geneva, St Moritz, Paris. In the French capital he meets Greek people of letters and the arts who have left Greece because of the civil war. He also meets and gets to know Pierre Reverdy, André Breton, David Gascoyne, Tristan Tzara, René Char, Pierre Emmanuel, Giuseppe Ungaretti, the painter Joan Miró and the critics of Greek origin Christian Zervos and E. Tériade. T.S. Eliot is in Paris in April and dedicates a copy of his book *The Family Reunion* to him.

**1949**   Becomes a founder member of the Parisian "Association International des Critiques d'Art". Gets to know the painters Pablo Picasso, Fernand Léger and Henri Matisse, and the sculptor Alberto Giacometti. He is obliged to stay in the French capital because the Greek consulate refuses to renew his passport.

1950   Makes the acquaintance of Jean Paul Sartre, Albert Camus, Henri Michaux and Philippe Soupault. The then Prime Minister of Greece Nicholas Plastiras gives orders for the renewal of his passport. Travels to Spain and London. Begins to compose *The Axion Esti*.

**1951**   Gives four talks on BBC radio in London. In Italy, meets the teacher Filippo Maria Pontani and the painter Giorgio de Chirico. Returns to

Athens, where another teacher, sent by Giuseppe Ungaretti, namely one Mario Vitti, who then becomes a translator and studier of his works, comes to meet him. At the end of the year the periodical *Verve*, entirely dedicated to Pablo Picasso, circulates in Paris. It contains an essay by Elytis entitled "Equivalences chez Picasso".

**1952** A collection of his poems, translated into Italian by Mario Vitti, circulates in Rome.

**1955** Writes the collection *Six and One Remorses for the Sky* in its initial form.

**1956** Jean Giraudoux's *Ondine* is presented at the National Theatre in Elytis' translation. Translates Brecht's *The Caucasian Chalk Circle*, which will be presented the following year at Karolos Koun's Art Theatre. It is the first theatrical work of Brecht to be presented in Greece.

**1958** Acquaintance and immediate friendship with Jean Genet. Starts to translate Genet's work *The Maids*.

**1960** Two of his books, *The Axion Esti* and *Six and One Remorses for the Sky,* circulate simultaneously in March. In July a collection of his poems in German translation by Barbara Schlorb and Antigone Kasolea circulates in Germany. He is awarded the State Poetry Prize. In London (and in 1961 in New York) Edmund Keeley and Philip

Sherard publish *Six Poets of Modern Greece*, containing poems by Elytis.

**1961** He becomes a regular member of the Comunità Europea degli Scrittori. From March to June he travels to the USA at the invitation of the State Department. His co-operation with the composer Mikis Theodorakis in setting *The Axion Esti* to music as an oratorio begins. He becomes acquainted with Yves Bonnefoy and Allen Ginsberg.

**1962** He travels by invitation to Moscow with Andreas Embirikos and Giorgos Theotokas. *Heroic and Elegiac Song for the Lost Second Lieutenant of Albania* is printed in Athens.

**1964** The musical setting of *The Axion Esti* is completed and is included in the Athens Festival programme. The Ministry to the Prime Minister refuses to allow it in the Odeon of Herodes Atticus and the work is premiered in the Rex cinema. Records of the musical setting are released simultaneously.

**1965** Travels to Bulgaria with Giorgios Theotokas at the invitation of the Union of Bulgarian Writers. On his return he is made Commander of the Order of the Phoenix by King Constantine.

**1966** New edition of his collection *Orientations*. Edmund Keeley's and Philip Sherrard's *Four*

*Greek Poets*, containing translations of poems by Cavafy, Seferis, Elytis and Nikos Gatsos is published in London.

1967    Travels to Egypt in February. Dictatorship proclaimed in Greece on the 21st of April. Elytis distances himself from all publicity.

1968    Karolos Koun's Art Theatre presents Jean Genet's *The Maids* in Elytis' translation. Pierre Emmanuel invites him to Paris to read his poems; Elytis refuses on account of the dictatorship. A selection of his poems in Vincenzo Rotolo's translation circulates in Palermo, Italy.

1969    Leaves for Paris. The *Axion Esti* in Günter Dietz's translation circulates in Germany.

1970    Stays in Cyprus for four months.

1971    Several books printed in Brussels in large format hand-written editions: the poem *The Monogram* for the Cypriot publisher L'oiseau, and in Athens the collections *The Light Tree and the Fourteenth Beauty* and *The Sovereign Sun*.

1972    Is pressed to accept the literature prize, which would be accompanied by a very large sum of money, instituted by the dictatorship. Goes into hiding to escape persuasion and compulsion. *The R's of Eros* and *The Monogram* are published in their first type-set Greek editions.

**1973** The poem "Villa Natacha" with an original drawing by Pablo Picasso is published by Tram Editions in Thessaloniki.

**1974** The dictatorship falls in July. For a few months Elytis is appointed chairman of the Greek State Radio and Television (EPT) and a member of the governing body of the National Theatre. At the same time, two of his books are published in the United States: *The Axion Esti*, translated by Edmund Keeley and G.P. Savvidis, and *The Sovereign Sun*, translated by Kimon Friar. Two new books of his appear in Athens: the poetry collection *Ta eterothali* (The Half-Siblings) and the volume of essays *Open Papers*.

**1975** Issue of the periodical *Books Abroad* dedicated to Elytis, including a long interview by Ivar Ivask.

**1976** Two new books of his circulate in Athens: *Second Writing*, a volume of translations of foreign poets, and the essay *The Spell of Papadiamandis*.

**1977** Declines invitation to become a member of the Athens Academy. "Poetry is a mission. It doesn't win prizes", he declares. François-Bernard Mâche's translation of *Six and One Remorses for the Sky* circulates in France.

**1978** In Thessaloniki Tram Editions bring out the essay *Report to Andreas Embirikos*. Elytis is granted an honorary doctorate by the School of Philosophy of Aristotle University Thessaloniki. *Maria Nephele* is published at the end of the year.

**1979**   He is awarded the Nobel Prize in Literature. *The Axion Esti* and *Six and One Remorses for the Sky* circulate in Sweden at the end of the year.

**1980**   Translations of his works are published (or reprinted) in Germany, France, Spain, Yugoslavia, Estonia, and Romania. In February he is awarded an honorary doctorate by the Sorbonne. Deposits his Nobel Prize gold medal in the Benaki Museum, Athens. Goes to Spain in October at the invitation of the then Prime Minister Adolfo Suárez. Is received by the royal couple, and welcomed enthusiastically by the University of Barcelona.

**1981**   New translations of his works abroad: Mexico, Hungary, Italy, Finland. *Maria Nephele* is translated in the United States and Germany. In November Elytis is awarded an honorary doctorate by the University of London.

**1982**   His new collection, *Three Poems under a Flag of Convenience*, circulates in the Spring. *Six and One Remorses for the Sky* is translated by Nina Angelidi and Nicolas Cocaro in Argentina.

**1983**   The New York periodical *The Charioteer* dedicates a multi-page issue to Elytis. The Lesbos Shipping Company names its new ship on the Piraeus-Mytilene line after Elytis. He is among the passengers on its maiden voyage, and is greeted with honour and enthusiasm when the ship arrives in Mytilene. *The Axion Esti* is translated in Norway and Argentina.

**1984** The volume *Sappho* circulates in Spring, "Reconstructed and rendered by Odysseus Elytis". New edition of his poems in Germany. In December another collection of his poems appears, *Journal of an Unseen April*.

**1985** The University of Padua in Italy circulates an honorary volume by the lecturer Filippo Maria Pontani entitled *Lirica greca da Archiloco a Elitis*. The poet's publications continue with two more books: his rendering into Modern Greek of the *Revelation* of St John, and *The Little Mariner*.

**1986** *Maria Nephele* published in Argentina in translation by Nina Angelidi–Spinelli and Horacio Castillo. A selection of his poems made by Olga Brouma is published in the United States. The volume *To domatio me tis eikones* (The Room with the Pictures), consisting of 44 illustrated compositions by the poet, circulates in Athens in November. Elytis is admitted to hospital in Athens, where he remains until January 1987 with a hematological complaint.

**1987** A translation of *The Axion Esti* circulates in France in March. In May the poet is given an honorary doctorate by La Sapienza University in Rome, and this occasions the publication of the volume *Omaggio a Odisseas Elitis*. In the same month he is similarly honoured by Athens University. *Three Poems under a Flag of Convenience* is translated into Dutch by Wim Bakker. A new publication appears in Athens: the volume *Krinagoras*; a Modern Greek version accompanied by the ancient text.

1988    New translations of his works in Argentina and the United States. In December a big exhibition for the poet is inaugurated in the Pompidou Centre, Paris, with many presentations, and with the publication of the volume *Odysseus Elytis: un méditerranéen universel*.

1989    The French state names him Commander of the Legion of Honour, its highest distinction for foreigners.

1990    The poet is again admitted to hospital in Athens. His book *Idiotiki odos* (Private Road), with 33 illustrations in Tempera, a watercolour, and twelve of his drawings, dedicated to Ioulita Iliopoulou, circulates. New translations of his works in other countries.

1991    The poem "Iouliou Logos" (Word of July), in a volume containing photographs of the poet as a child, is privately printed, not for publication, under the direction of Ioulita Iliopoulou. An exhibition of the Greek surrealists is inaugurated at the Pompidou Centre, Paris. New translations of his works in Iraq, The Netherlands and Germany. On the second of November the poet reaches the age of 80: a matter of particular public note in Greece. This coincides with the publication of a new collection of poetry, *The Oxopetra Elegies*.

1992  In the summer an exhibition of pictorial compositions by Elytis and sculptures by Alberto Giacometti is inaugurated at the Museum of Modern Art in Andros, and a one-day conference about the poet is held. To mark the occasion the volume *Andros 1982* was published, under the supervision of Ioulita Iliopoulou, containing pictorial compositions by the poet. New translations of his works abroad (Bahrein and Italy). The volume *Carte Blanche* circulates, with prose texts from 1972-1992.

1993  On the 10th of February he is again taken into hospital in Athens. The serious state of his health causes concern throughout Greece. He will stay in hospital until the middle of July.

1994  From the 25th to the 29th of June, Ioannina University and the Cultural Centre of Kos hold an international conference about Elytis in Kos.

1995   Two new books circulate in December: the
       poetry collection *West of Sorrow* and the volume
       *O kipos me tis aftapates* (The Garden of Self-
       delusions); prose works with 49 illustrations.

1996   On the afternoon of the 18th of March Elytis
       dies in his flat. He is buried in the Athens First
       Cemetery without any great pomp, according
       to his wishes. His will was opened on the 29th
       of March, the sole beneficiary being Ioulita Ilio-
       poulou. The volume of short prose pieces *2χ7ε*
       circulates on his birthday, the 2nd of November.

# Book-length translations of Elytis' work in English

*The Sovereign Sun, Selected Poems,* Translated with an Introduction and notes by Kimon Friar, Philadelphia: Temple University Press, 1974; Also Newcastle upon Tyne: Bloodaxe Books, 1990.

*To Axion Esti. The Axion Esti* (bilingual), Translated and annotated by Edmund Keeley and George Savidis, Pittsburgh: University of Pittsburgh Press, 1974; London: Anvil Press, 1980 and 2007 (English only).

*Selected Poems*, Chosen and introduced by Edmund Keeley and Philip Sherrard, Translated by Edmund Keeley, Philip Sherrard, George Savidis, John Stathatos and Nanos Valaoritis, New York: The Viking Press and Penguin Books, 1981; Also London: Anvil Press, 1981 and 2007.

*Maria Nephele. A Poem in Two Voices*, Translated by Athan Anagnostopoulos, Boston: Houghton Mifflin, 1981.

*What I Love. Selected Poems of Odysseas Elytis*, Translated by Olga Broumas, Washington: Copper Canyon Press, 1986.

*Six and One Remorses for the Sky (and other poems)*, Translated by Jeffrey Carson, Helsinki: Eurographica, 1985.

*The Little Mariner*, Translated by Olga Broumas, Washington: Copper Canyon Press, 1988.

*Open Papers*, Translated by Olga Broumas and T. Begley, Washington: Copper Canyon Press, 1995.

*The Oxopetra Elegies* (bilingual), Translated by David Connolly, Amsterdam: Harwood Academic Publishers, 1996.

*The Collected Poems of Odysseus Elytis*, Translated by Jeffrey Carson and Nikos Sarris, Introduction and notes by Jeffrey Carson, Baltimore: The Johns Hopkins University Press, 1997.

*Journal of an Unseen April* (bilingual), Translated by David Connolly, Athens: Ypsilon Books, 1998.

*Carte Blanche. Selected Writings*, Translated by David Connolly, Amsterdam: Harwood Academic Publishers, 1999.

*The Oxopetra Elegies & West of Sorrow*, Translated with an Introduction by David Connolly, Cambridge, MA: Harvard University Press, 2012.

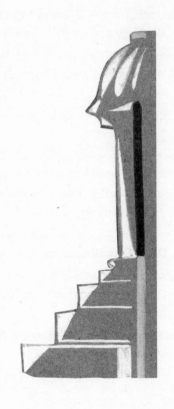

# READ THE MODERN GREEK CLASSICS

CONSTANTINE P. CAVAFY
## Selected Poems
Translated by David Connolly

ANDREAS LASKARATOS
## Reflexions
Translated by Simon Darragh

ALEXANDROS PAPADIAMANDIS
## Fey Folk
Translated by David Connolly

GEORGE SEFERIS
## Novel and Other Poems
Translated by Roderick Beaton

GEORGIOS VIZYENOS
## Thracian Tales
Translated by Peter Mackridge

GEORGIOS VIZYENOS
## Moskov Selim
Translated by Peter Mackridge

NIKIFOROS VRETTAKOS
## Selected Poems
Translated by David Connolly

## Rebetika
Songs from the Old Greek Underworld
Translated by Katharine Butterworth & Sara Schneider

www.aiora.gr